ALABAMA

TWENTIETH CENTURY

Project Manager: SY FELDMAN
Book Art Layout: CARMEN FORTUNATO
Album Art Direction: SUSAN EADDY / BILL BRUNT
Photography: PETER NASH

© 1999 WARNER BROS. PUBLICATIONS
All Rights Reserved

Any duplication, adaptation or arrangement of the compositions
contained in this collection requires the written consent of the Publisher.
No part of this book may be photocopied or reproduced in any way without permission.
Unauthorized uses are an infringement of the U.S. Copyright Act and are punishable by law.

CONTENTS

TWENTIETH CENTURY

Words and Music by
DON SCHLITZ and
CHRIS A.T. CUMMINGS

© 1999 NEW DON SONGS/NEW HAYES MUSIC and CPL, INC./KE-CHING MUSIC
All Rights Reserved

Verse 4:

twen - ti - eth cen - tu - ry___ was - n't all___ that long,

mp

just a hun - dred years___ has come and gone.

cresc.

We

can't go back e - ven if we try,___ so I'll just smile_ and_ wave good - bye.___ To

mf

see it leav - in' makes___ me kind - a sad.

It was a

time like no one else___ has ev - er had.___

Aw, the

Repeat ad lib. and fade

Verse 2:
Yeah, the twentieth century was quite a ride.
We had to learn to see the other side.
We had demonstrations and liberations,
Great depressions and good vibrations,
And doors that once were closed were opened wide.
Oh, the twentieth century was quite a ride.
(To Bridge 1:)

Verse 3:
Yeah, the twentieth century was a heck of a show.
We all had our fifteen minutes, don't you know?
Assembly lines, celebrities,
The spotlight shined on you and me.
And everybody got a standin' O.
Yeah, the twentieth century was a heck of a show.
(To Bridge 2:)

(GOD MUST HAVE SPENT)
A LITTLE MORE TIME ON YOU

Words and Music by
CARL STURKEN and EVAN ROGERS

© 1998 SONGS OF UNIVERSAL, INC. and BAYJUN BEAT MUSIC
All Rights Administered by SONGS OF UNIVERSAL, INC.
All Rights Reserved

(God Must Have Spent) A Little More Time on You - 5 - 4
PF9920

12

Verse 2:
In all of creation,
All things great and small,
You are the one that surpasses them all.
More precious than
Any diamond or pearl;
They broke the mold
When you came in this world.
And I'm trying hard to figure it out,
Just how I ever did without
The warmth of your smile.
The heart of a child
That's deep inside,
Leaves me purified.
(To Chorus:)

(God Must Have Spent) A Little More Time on You - 5 - 5
PF9920

I'M IN THAT KIND OF MOOD

Words and Music by
RANDY OWEN, TEDDY GENTRY,
GREG FOWLER and RONNIE ROGERS

I'm in That Kind of Mood - 5 - 1
PF9920

© 1999 SONY/ATV SONGS LLC and ROUTE SIX MUSIC
All Rights for SONY/ATV SONGS LLC Administered by SONY/ATV MUSIC PUBLISHING,
8 Music Square West, Nashville, TN 37203
All Rights Reserved   Used by Permission

I'm in That Kind of Mood - 5 - 3
PF9920

Verse 2:
It's been a while since we've been out.
It's overdue, baby, ain't no doubt, you know,
Ain't it so?
It's feelin' like our first date.
To tell the truth now, honey, I can't wait to go.
And I think you know.
Well, tonight it's just us two.
And baby I want you.
(To Chorus:)

WE MADE LOVE

Words and Music by
TOM DOUGLAS and BILLY KIRSCH

We Made Love - 4 - 1
PF9920

© 1997, 1999 SONY/ATV SONGS LLC and HAMSTEIN CUMBERLAND MUSIC/KID JULIE MUSIC
All Rights for SONY/ATV SONGS LLC Administered by SONY/ATV MUSIC PUBLISHING,
8 Music Square West, Nashville, TN 37203
All Rights Reserved   Used by Permission

Verse 2:
Through the lonely that divides us,
And I can feel you reachin' from the other side.
Let's tear this wall down and start over,
And get back to, oh, that simple life.
(To Chorus:)

LIFE'S TOO SHORT TO LOVE THIS FAST

Words and Music by
RANDY OWEN, GARY BAKER
and FRANK J. MYERS

© 1999 SONY /ATV SONGS LLC and
ZOMBA ENTERPRISES INC./SWEAR BY IT MUSIC/JOSH NICK MUSIC
(All Rights Administered by ZOMBA ENTERPRISES INC.)
All Rights Reserved

THEN WE REMEMBER

Words and Music by
DON COOK and JOHN JARVIS

Moderately ♩ = 96

1. You've got your se - crets. Girl, I've got mine.__ We're fall - in' a - part__ one glance__

Then We Remember - 4 - 1
PF9920

© 1987, 1999 SONY/ATV TUNES LLC/SONY/ATV SONGS LLC
All Rights Administered by SONY/ATV MUSIC PUBLISHING,
8 Music Square West, Nashville, TN 37203
All Rights Reserved   Used by Permission

Verses 2 & 3:

_____ at a time._____ Night af-ter night,_____ act-in' like

strang - ers._____ 2. Out of e - mo - tion,_
3. *See additional lyrics*

no-thing to say._____ I brush your shoul - der but you_____ turn a - way._____

No-bod-y tries,_____ no-bod-y's chang - ing._____

Who'll be the first to say it's real - ly the end?_____
4. *Inst. solo ad lib. . . .*

Verse 3:
One night of passion won't stop the pain.
Back to the same old feelin' again.
Time after time, is it worth savin'?
Who'll be the first to say it's really the end?
Who's gonna walk out the door?
How did we let it get so out of control?
Our hearts can't take anymore.
(To Chorus:)

LITTLE THINGS

Words and Music by
RANDY GREEN, TEDDY GENTRY,
GREG FOWLER, JOHN JARRARD and BUDDY CANNON

Little Things - 4 - 1
PF9920

© 1999 SONY/ATV SONGS LLC, SONY/ATV TUNES LLC, MISS BLYSS MUSIC and BILL N BUD MUSIC
All Rights Administered by SONY/ATV MUSIC PUBLISHING,
8 Music Square West, Nashville, TN 37203
All Rights Reserved   Used by Permission

Verse 3:
Lyin' in the bed beside you,
Touchin' in the middle of the night.
No, you don't have to do any talkin'
To tell me everything is all right.
(To Chorus:)

MIST OF DESIRE

Words and Music by
JEFF COOK

Mist of Desire - 4 - 1
PF9920

© 1999 SONY/ATV SONGS LLC
All Rights Administered by SONY/ATV MUSIC PUBLISHING,
8 Music Square West, Nashville, TN 37203
All Rights Reserved   Used by Permission

Verse 2:
I feel the love when we touch;
I can see it in your face.
I get lost in the shadows of your warm embrace.
And you rush into my arms.
My emotions run wild,
And we're off to a love world
In a mist of desire.
(To Chorus:)

SMALL STUFF

Words and Music by
MARK COLLIE, HILLARY KANTER
and EVEN STEVENS

Small Stuff - 6 - 1
PF9920

© 1999 ESP MUSIC (Adm. by MUSIC & MEDIA INTERNATIONAL)
All Rights Reserved   Used by Permission

Small Stuff - 6 - 5
PF9920

Repeat ad lib. and fade

Verse 2:
There's a little bitty hole in the ceiling above,
Sometimes the rain drips down on our temple of love.
We have to put a pot smack dab in the middle of the bed.
Somebody hit my car at the diner last night,
Had to drive it home with one taillight.
When I went out this morning, the engine was dead.
That's small stuff; we don't sweat the small stuff.
(To Chorus:)

TOO MUCH LOVE

Words and Music by
RANDY OWEN and GREG FOWLER

Too Much Love - 3 - 1
PF9920

© 1999 SONY/ATV SONGS LLC
All Rights for SONY/ATV SONGS LLC Administered by SONY/ATV MUSIC PUBLISHING,
8 Music Square West, Nashville, TN 37203
All Rights Reserved   Used by Permission

Verse 2:
Silence can be deafening
When you don't make a sound.
At times, you make me wonder
Why you want me around.
(To Chorus:)

Bridge 2:
There are rocky roads,
And it's touch and go,
And there are times to be alone.
But there's something deeper
That we can't explain;
It's an everlasting flame.
(To Chorus:)

WRITE IT DOWN IN BLUE

Words and Music by
RANDY OWEN, TEDDY GENTRY,
GREG FOWLER and RONNIE ROGERS

© 1999 SONY/ATV SONGS LLC and ROUTE SIX MUSIC
All Rights Administered by SONY/ATV MUSIC PUBLISHING,
8 Music Square West, Nashville, TN 37203
All Rights Reserved   Used by Permission

Verse 2:
What you are feeling, you just can't explain.
Oh, you got your reasons, now you just can't change.
And there's no way to hide it 'cause, baby, I can see.
So, if you can't say it then do this for me.
(To Chorus:)

I LOVE YOU ENOUGH TO LET YOU GO

Words and Music by
RANDY OWEN, GARY BAKER
and FRANK J. MYERS

1. I've rehearsed_ this day_ a thousand times._ I've played_ this scene_ out in my mind._ You spread_ your wings,_ you need_ to fly._ It breaks my heart_ to say

2.3. *See additional lyrics*

I Love You Enough to Let You Go - 4 - 1
PF9920

© 1999 SONY/ATV SONGS LLC and ZOMBA ENTERPRISES INC./SWEAR BY IT MUSIC/JOSH NICK MUSIC
(All Rights Administered by ZOMBA ENTERPRISES INC.)
All Rights Reserved

54

Verse 2:
My mind goes back to memories
Of pony rides upon my knee,
First day of school, your brand new bike,
And football games on Friday night.
And through the years I've watched you grow
And I love you enough to let you go.
(To Chorus:)

Verse 3:
So many things I wanna say;
You'll meet new friends, you'll be okay.
I'll pray for you out on your own,
But don't forget your way back home.
And though I may not let it show,
I love you enough to let you go.
(To Chorus:)

Alabama
Deluxe Anthology
(PF9738)

Without question, Alabama is one of the best country bands of all time with more than 40 No. 1 country singles and more than 45 million albums sold. The 52 songs in this career-spanning Deluxe Anthology are:

Angels Among Us • Born Country • Can't Keep a Good Man Down • The Cheap Seats • Close Enough to Perfect • The Closer You Get • Dancin', Shaggin' on the Boulevard • Dixieland Delight • Down Home • Face to Face • Fallin' Again • Feels So Right • Forever Is as Far as I'll Go • Forty Hour Week (For a Livin') • Give Me One More Shot • Here We Are • High Cotton • Hometown Honeymoon • If You're Gonna Play in Texas (You Gotta Have a Fiddle in the Band) • If I Had You • I'm in a Hurry (And I Don't Know Why) • In Pictures • It Works • Jukebox in My Mind • Lady Down on Love • Love in the First Degree • The Maker Said Take Her • Mountain Music • Old Flame • Once Upon a Lifetime • Pass It On Down • Reckless • Roll On (Eighteen Wheeler) • Sad Lookin' Moon • Say I • She Ain't Your Ordinary Girl • She and I • Song of the South • Southern Star • T.L.C. A.S.A.P. • Take a Little Trip • Take Me Down • Tar Top • Tennessee River • Then Again • There's a Fire in the Night • There's No Way • Touch Me When We're Dancing • We Can't Love Like This Anymore • When We Make Love • Why Lady Why • "You've Got" the Touch.